For John and Kerry Fix—D.D.M.

For the many special teachers who helped me find my way—J.B.H.

Text © 2005 Dandi Daley Mackall.
Illustrations © 2005 Jenny B Harris.
© 2005 Standard Publishing, Cincinnati, Ohio.
A division of Standex International Corporation.
All rights reserved. Printed in China.
Project editor: Robin Stanley.
Cover and interior design: Marissa Bowers.
Scripture quotations are taken from The Holy Bible, New Living Translation, copyright © 1996.
Used by permission of Tyndale House Publishers, Inc., Wheaton, IL. 60189.
All rights reserved.
12 11 10 09 08 07 06 05   9 8 7 6 5 4 3 2 1
ISBN 0-7847-1652-8

Library of Congress Cataloging-in-Publication Data on file.

Jesus said, "Go tell the world," so I'VE GOT A JOB TO DO

Written by Dandi Daley Mackall   Pictures by Jenny B Harris

Standard
PUBLISHING
Bringing The Word to Life™

Cincinnati, Ohio

Jesus loves the world;
the Bible tells us so.

Now he's back in heaven,
and he tells us, "Go!
People need a Savior.
Tell them, 'God loves you!'"

So I've got a job to do.

If I walk to school, or I ride the bus,
I can tell my friends Jesus died for us.
If the driver asks, I can tell her, too.

I've got a job to do.

Will my life show Christ in the way I love?
Will I help the world like my God above?
At a party, park, or a barbeque . . .

I've got a job to do.

I will move in faith when I have a hunch,
ask a lonely kid if he'll share my lunch.
I can bless our food, maybe bless us, too.

I've got a job to do.

I could ask my friend,
"Come to church with me?"

I might even ask her whole family!
'Cause we need each other, and you know that's true.

I've got a job to do.

Jesus came and told his disciples, "...Go and make disciples of all the nations."
Matthew 28:18, 19

When I'm at the beach with a friend of mine,
and we stand in awe of the bright sunshine,
I'll say, "Thank you, God, for this awesome view!"

I've got a job to do.

Jesus came and told his disciples, "...Go and make disciples of all the nations."

Matthew 28:18, 19

I have friends and family that I love a lot.
And though some know Jesus, maybe some do not.
I want all of THEM up in heaven, too.

So I've got a job to do.

Jesus came and told his disciples, "...Go and make disciples of all the nations." Matthew 28:18, 19

When I'm all grown up
I could be a clown . . .

or an airplane pilot
flying upside down.

I might tend the ponies in a petting zoo.

I'll still have a job to do.

From the highest mountain, to the valleys low,
far beyond the sea, everywhere I go.
From the tip of Iceland, out to Timbuktu,

I've got a job to do.

Jesus came and told his disciples, "...Go and make disciples of all the nations."
Matthew 28:18, 19

What if no one listens? What if no one cares?
Then I'll talk to Jesus in my daily prayers,
and I'll trust in HIM for the follow through.

'Cause I've got a job to do.

Jesus came and told his disciples, "...Go and make disciples of all the nations."
Matthew 28:18, 19

It's the greatest message—he's the Living Word.
It's the best Good News that you ever heard!
I could never hide it, if I wanted to.

I've got a job to do.

Jesus came and told his disciples, "...Go and make disciples of all the nations."
Matthew 28:18, 19

Now it doesn't matter if I'm kind of small,
for the Great Commission goes to one and all.
When I go with Jesus, he will see me through!

I've got a job to do.

Matthew 28:18-20

Jesus came and told his disciples,
"I have been given complete authority in heaven and on earth.

Therefore,
go and make
disciples
of all the nations,

baptizing them in the name of the Father
and the Son and the Holy Spirit.

Teach these new disciples to obey all the
commands I have given you.

And be sure of this:

I am with you always,
even to the end of the age."